I've been havin' dreams...

I'm not sleep. Yet, I'm not awake.

I've been havin' dreams...

I'm not sleep. Yet, I'm not awake.

Tigerlilystar

PenFire
Publishing

PenFire Publishing
Kansas City, MO
penfirepublishing.com

Copyright © 2020 by Tigerlilystar

All rights reserved. No part of this book may be reproduced, scanned, or distributed in any printed or electronic form, including information storage and retrieval systems, without permission. Please do not participate in or encourage piracy of copyrighted materials in violation of the author's rights. Please purchase only authorized editions.

First Edition: December 2020

ISBN: 978-1-952838-03-3

Library of Congress Control Number: 2020920213

This book is a work of fiction. Names, characters, places, dates, and incidents are products of the author's imagination or are used fictitiously, satirically, or as parody. Any resemblance to actual persons, living or dead, business establishments, events, or locales is entirely coincidental.

10 9 8 7 7 5 4 3 3 1

Design, Layout, Edits: Sheri Hall & Brooke Hawkins

Dedication

This is mine. I shall thank how I want. God. No more to express.

McKenzie. Frog. My dream come true. I'm able to be my full self because you've never hesitated in your own glory.
I love you.

Wokee. Everything I chased in my head? You found nets to make the cap-ture easier. Consistency. Words. Songs. Safety. Tate.

Sheri. I'm inspired. I feel like you are fluent in the language of me. I keep crying. You call it birth. I find solace with you.

This is also for those attached to 4 East. I'm not all that you think I am. Or what you would like me to be I'm sure. But I am exactly myself and firm in it because of each one of you. I love you. Extended dedication to the one that help saved my eyes and my life.

Deadpool.

Black Imagination. Mamas Quilt. My Brothers & Sisters. Worship Culture. TAP OUT. The Wade's. The Artist Community Project. Quez Presents. NeoEmoSoul. Soul Sessions. Team BGV. SQUAD. The Whispers. SKATZ. The Black Repertory of Kansas City. Square 1 Therapy. Champwork. 3 Piece & Biskuit. Go Hard. SweeTwists. Pink Matter.

Monroe.
LLC.
Fly High.

Everything I've written I've felt. Everything I've felt I am. So this is for me. Just Angel. Tigerlilystar.

Contents

Dedication 5

A. Labyrinth 10
    What's Wrong With My Love 12
    Ring 14
    Curiosity 16
    SENRYU 19
    TANKA 20
    As We Lay 21
    Phact 23
    I Have Questions 24
    Waiting 25
    Phact Is Liphe 26
    Beyond Until 28
    Hey Love, ... 29
    Healing 30
    12019 33
    Good Morning 35

B. Wet Dreams 38
    June 18 40
    SENRYU 41
    TANKA 42
    My Fantasy 43

C. Nightmare on Elm St. 44
    Acknowledgement of Misery 46
    Missing You 48
    Masters-So 49
    Rav'n 50
    Silence 51
    SENRYU 52
    Take it Back! 53
    9-29-01 54

Shook 55
This Ain't Oz 57

D. Ror·schach test 59
    Lend A Hand 61
    Ok Then 62
    SENRYU 63
    TANKA 64
    The Question 65
    Baby Tate... 66
    Difficult 67
    A Missing Angel 68
    8.24.01 69
    ESPN Balla-Wanna-Be 70
    Here 71
    Dragonfly 72
    Women 73
    Leaving Home 75
    Discovery 76
    Not Quite a Bucket List 77
    My Origin Story 79

A. Labyrinth

lab·y·rinth
/ˈlab(ə)ˌrinTH/

noun

a complicated irregular network of
passages or paths in which it is
difficult to find one's way; a maze.
"A labyrinth of passages and secret chambers."

What's Wrong With My Love

What's wrong with my love?
It causes thunderstorms
And destruction,
Trees exploding,
Lightning that rips apart the sky
And stings sleep salted eyes
That's what it does

> Erupts Earth's crusted layer
> With mighty gushing winds,
> Cold, angry rain
> Making children sprint from
> Solace laden blankets
> And rooms devoid of comfort,
> Sliding into the home base
> Of mommas bed

What's wrong with my love?
It conspires.
Not on purpose though.
I mean, it didn't intend to kill Lincoln
It exploded into the back of his head,
Spilling brain from his nose and lips.
That's what it did.

> Watergate was an accident, I promise!
> And when my love erased the messages
> On the white house answering machine
> Warning us about 9/11,
> I thought it was just another
> Irritating phone call from Cleo
> Bothering me about a free reading!

Is my love so bad
That it killed all the Dodo's and Quaggas?
Suddenly made all the dragons
And unicorns imaginary
But kept Shar-pei,
Jerry Curls and Jeffrey Dahmer?

That's what it did.

>   What's wrong with my love?
>   It causes starving children
>   In 3rd world countries
>   To have big ole heads,
>   Skinny arms and legs,
>   And protruding stomachs.
>   My love makes them sickly.

My love causes catastrophes
Like Hurricane Bob, and Andy.
Caused the world to be flat
And turned Narcissus into a flower
While staring vainly at lake waters.
My love caused World War II.
That's what it does.

>   My love was the tree that hit Bono.
>   My love was the ground beneath Christopher
>   Reaves and the horse that threw him.
>   It was simultaneously the movie Glitter
>   And the beating of Rodney King.
>   It eats up goodness and turns it
>   Into something rotted and vile.

What's wrong with my love?
It causes confusion and dismay;
Brings on guilt, pity, pain,
Monsters, mourning, and deceit.
It causes man to wonder *what good is he*
Making them hate and shudder within.
That's what it does.

>   My love rewards the unfaithful
>   While the genuine fall apart.
>   That's what's wrong with my love.

Ring

why does HE feel obligated
to talk to me when
HE talks to SHE?

SHE captivated him for
many days and evenings
bringing closeness to
THEIR friendship

with HE on the phone
i suddenly feel
hands on my shoulders
a kiss on the cheek
frequent embraces
that cause ME to wonder
what effect SHE has
on we

is it motivated comfort
to keep ME assured?
or is it his own nervousness
that put him in an ultra-loving frenzy

HE looks at me inquisitively and
talks to HER
looks at me while
listening to HER
asking ME if i am ok

in actuality
i just wish HE
would leave me alone
when on the phone with SHE

HE already knows i disapprove
why make it worse by
adding my presence to
a realm of feelings
where i'd rather not be

i hate the feeling taking hold of me
a strange feeling
like i have no control
of the actions and events
that surround me,
    DJ, Cue Floetry song #5 "It's getting late"

i hear a pause in the air
suddenly the presence of SHE
is gone

HE is back
the world is where it should be

once again
it's just ME
until
the phone rings

Curiosity

I see you
Watching me
Approvingly
Inquisitively

I mean
What else can you see but
Miss Divine
Nubian perfection
Q u e e n

I don't understand
Why you can't
Step up to the plate
And verbally appreciate
Openly reveal that
You. Want. Me.

I know what those glances mean
All those stupid jokes
Between you and me
And true
I know that girl I seen
Ain't just a buddy … *can't be*
She be yo *regular* thing

Don't confuse it
I don't *hate*
I'm just trying to see
Where I fit
In the scheme of things

Quite honestly
If given the proper opportunity
I would merge onto the highway
Of uncertainty
Cruise control a steady pace
Not saying a damn thang
Swerving this built better

Than Bentley body
Past your face

On the real
What would there be left to say?
Either you is or you ain't
M y   B a b y
>   *I'm getting way ahead of myself*
>   *I keep forgetting*
>   *You ain't even stepped yet*

If you ain't
I will find somebody who is
Somebody that will
Rock my body
Worship each wrinkle
Ingrained in my brain
Immerse themselves
In my fragrant locs

But…
I s e e   y o u
Watching me
Approvingly
Inquisitively

And yeah
I'm feeling you
I mean
Maybe its my carnal mind
Seeing the sex
In your deep-set eyes
That lights the fire and
Hits back through mine
Your mahogany skin
And quiet demeanor
Gets me every time

When you speak to me
You seem to see through me
The world fades
And it's just you and me

At least that's how you make me feel
Just keepin' it real
It would kill me
To miss a chance
Because of my quiet stance
Then I sit and think
    What the hell am I doing?
    I have no clue!

But…
You gotta know I want you
A l l .   O f .   Y o u .

SENRYU

I

Totally in love
Our bond is unbreakable
I belong to you

II

Take my hand in yours
Recognizing my heart's depth
Timelessness abounds

III

Iridescent glow
Contagious you are to me
I sleep in wonder

IV

I love the way you
Make haste joining me in bed
Sleep breeze on my face

V

He gives of himself
Whenever he is needed
Please know I'm grateful

TANKA

His name I can't say.
He is my soulmate and friend.
He listens to me.
Consistent. He gives freely.
I am forever grateful.

As We Lay

I watch him
In his slumber
Mouth fully agape

The sounds that escape
This revving engine
Driven by your
Morning breath breeze
Trading spaces with
Mumbles and grinding teeth

I should be sleep
But your stillness is
Absolute
I thought myself alone

Eyes snap open
And you are still there
Chest rising and falling
In time
Danceless beat

I nestle closer
Removing any space
Back against torso
Footpads pressed
Against leg

You don't budge
Just get louder
Like a
Dodge Challenger
Racing on I-70
You are that loud
But I'm used to it
It is solace
ASMR

You are darling

Face relaxed
No worry
In the brow

I reach
Pull your arm
Round myself
Close my eyes
Whisper a prayer
Then join you

Sleep

Phact

Life is such a funny game, all I want is your participation.

I want so badly that you want me too.
I want so badly that you love me too.
I want so badly.
You.

Your power causes a glow.
It's a touch so sweet.
Not even sure if you know
How your hands affect me.
Almost as swift
As an angel's flight
Your hands graze
Against mine.
I laid in your arms
and felt your essence.
I sighed at the softness of
Your breath against my neck.
I closed my eyes
And felt your strength.
You saw me beyond my faults,
Beyond my mistakes
And I was still, in the moment.

God,
I love the way you feel against me.
Damn,
I crave your presence

I want so badly that you want me too.
I want so badly that you love me too.
I want so badly.
You.

I Have Questions

Is it wrong of me to want to be put on a pedestal?
Is it bad to want attention?

Can you wake up and just think of me?
Can the dreams you have of me affect your sleep?

Please???

Can you love me enough to need me?
Can your love for me amount to more than infinity?

Am I asking,
        Asking,
                Asking,
                        Too much?
                                I need you to look at me, lovingly.

Could you love me?
See me at my worst?

See me when I just woke up and call it beauty?
Die on the inside and cry on the outside from the lack of me?

Please???

Can you see my smile as art and my voice as an unchained melody?
Can you watch me walk away and wish to control me like a cd player?
        Repeat,
                Repeat,
                        Repeat!
                              Huh baby? Is that really so wrong?

                                                Maybe.

Waiting

I close my eyes and think of you
Imagining that I am with you
Dreaming that I can feel you
It's cool though; I will be soon
Can't wait to feel those lips of yours
Pretty brown eyes that I adore
So lonely I can't take no more
Our time apart will soon be gone
Setting sun will bring new dawn
It feels so right it can't be wrong
Not much longer
No distance keeps my love from you
Life's biggest trials
We've made it through
All obstacles, we'll make it through
God knows how much I want you
This loneliness,
We got this too!

Phact Is Liphe

I consider you beautiful
No matter what anyone else says
Your beauty is unmeasurable
No matter what you say
Just the thought of seeing you
Causes me to worry
Fiddle with my hair
Check between my teeth
Turnabout in my mirror
Just to see
Of the image of me
Reflects the wonder
You say is in me
I find it funny
You tilt your head to the side
Gazing at me like
I'm the most exquisite
Art piece

I consider you beautiful
No matter what anyone else says
I can't help but to realize
That it's not just your nutmeg skin
That cause my head to spin
Or the length and thickness
Of those lashes
Surrounding oceans of love
That capture my soul
Making me feel whole
Not only the words
That spill from your lips
But, the excited rush, heated flush
Obtained by one kiss
I am moved by you
Moved by not only what you do
But moved by what you are to me
I am in love with
The possibility of a creation
Such as you

Co-existing in a world that
Allows me to
Abide in it
You,
Well…
You bring joy to a place
Where sorrow once resided
Fire to a spirit once grazed
By dampened hopes

I consider you beautiful
No matter what anyone else says
Closing my eyes thinking of you
Music surrounds me
Touching the hair that lines your lip
And rests upon your chin
How sexy it feels against my face
I long to grab hold and
Intertwine my fingers in
Each and every loc that
Blesses your shoulders
Carrying the decadence of
Shea and amber
Inhaling is oh so good
I lay against the strength of you
Revel in the safety of your arms
God's rays surround you
As you provide me with endless love
And constant sensuality
I love the way you hold me

I consider you beautiful
No matter what anyone else says
Your beauty is unmeasurable
No matter what you say

Beyond Until

i love it when
you hold me
and it feels
you wont let go
your eyes capture
mine saying that
you'll want me
forever
but baby
you make my day
when you say
you will love me
beyond until

you say you
require my breath
to sustain
and i am moved when
you kiss me soft
but darling
you make my day
when you say
you will love me
beyond until

Hey Love,

I want to feel your love
And experience it in many ways
I've reacted to its presence
Every single day
I see beams of moonlight melodies
Swim seas of twilight dreams
Your effervescent love
Stings each valve and heart string
Fills each beat with love songs
Unchained melodies intertwined
With promises of brand-new joyous memories
Awaiting mad consumption of your reality
And praying the totality of your beauty
Manifests itself to me
Sincerely, truly and deeply,
Your love envelops me
To be blessed with an extra day to love thee
Would cause a single hour to elapse into
A labyrinth of love
    Eternally,
          Me

Healing

I pray
I cry
I love
I fuck

I pray
I close my eyes or leave them open
I say them in my head or write them down
It's easier to write them down
God can hear it no matter how I do it
Even if it doesn't start with "Lord…"
He knows I'm speaking to him before I do
Sometimes it helps
Sometimes it doesn't
Sometimes I feel a mighty touch
A response and answer
I feel redeemed and filled
Other times I feel empty
Like I'm too far out of God's reach
Like I'm too far out of God's concern
But I do it anyway
Just in case
I know it's important
I know I'm important
Prayer heals

I cry
I cry a lot
I cry when I'm happy
I cry when Im sad
I cry from too much laughter
I cry when I can't fight
I cry when I do fight
I cry when I bleed
I cry from the thoughts of
   Wanting others to bleed
I cry for my child when
   She doesn't know she should
I cry for my ex-husband
   I know he will have regrets and it will be too late

I cry and I release everything
    That is too much to keep inside
    And it makes everything so much better
The issues may still be present
But the release is needed
And I never will let anyone tell me I can't cry
Crying heals

I love
I love so hard
    Immensely
    It's stressful at times
To love and love and love
And not receive the same in return
I've learned to accept that I have a gift
    I'm different
It's something that has always resonated within
I was built to love
I was created to heal others with my love
It's not always returned with the same intensity
    If even at all
But it's a gift that I'm required to give
It's what I am
I am love
I accept it
Love heals

I fuck
This is the fun part
The part most don't know
The part that I only share with those able
    To keep up and stay quiet
I'm good at it
I'm curious
I'm giving
I can tighten and I can expand
I am soft and delicate
I am resilient and strong
I can give demands without uttering a single word
I can take orders and follow through with every one
I'm sensual
I'm carefree

I'm open to every one of my senses
I'm as loving as I am ruthless
I crave and I am insatiable
Touch rejuvenates me
It provides and unexplainable energy
    That can not be compared
Fucking heals

I pray
I cry
I love
I fuck

12019

A dimly lit room
    hosted voices for
    a night full of rhythm
    a night filled with song
Speakers pound out
    beats
    for feet to move
    bodies sway
    hips   hands   motions
All this provides the
    setting of the least
    anticipated
    plot line
A story for generations
    to come
    a love story
    a meeting of two hearts
The pulse of two souls
    a journey
    unlike
    any other
Nothing prepared either
    for the slight graze
    of hand
    in passing
Nothing prepared either
    for the surprise in
    the step back
    to touch again
More pressure
    intended
    purposeful
    fingers clutch
Stride stops
    world stops
    heart
    stops
Everything is still
    music is no longer

      people disappear
      in a moment
In a settling of
      the connection
      eyes meet
      air stills
Left hand
      right arm
      pulls back
      like fire at first
Draws back to be
      consumed again
      damn the fire
      burn me whole
Eyes meet
      caught
      confusion
      desire
Something else
      can't speak
      mumbled words
      apologies uttered
Embarrassment
      takes over
      once again shy
      but not
Strength draws
      in fabric
      connection seals fate
      music returns reality
People return
      light goes from the gold
      flame of heat
      unexplained

We return back to the dimly lit room

Good Morning

I woke up this morning, and everything was different. I opened my eyes, and for the first time, my breathing was steady. I didn't squint my eyes and wait for the reality of my lonely surroundings, or dark reminders of past hurt, to press down upon me. There was no clenching of my pillows to my face to stifle the screams I often felt rising every single time the last of my six alarms went off. There was none of that. Ok, I did squint, just a little. Old habits die hard. But this time, there were no alarms. It's like my internal clock was aware of the change within. I opened my eyes fully and shifted from my side to my back, letting my fingertips creep across the bedding to the right of me. They only stopped their journey when they touched skin. Skin that wasn't mine but belonged to me. I let them linger for only a moment. Just long enough to make sure I was awake, and this was my existence. I was no longer alone.

For clarification's sake, the presence of a warm body in the bed isn't the only thing that changed my morning rituals from doom to, well, the complete opposite. But all I ever wanted was to *actually* have all the things that made me, ME (My angst, my talent, my laughter, the strange way I look at the world and choose to love…). I wanted to be received, appreciated, loved, and needed; cherished like I cherish my daughter. But different? I don't want to be loved like a child. Well, include the unconditional love part, and I will grab at that! What am I saying?

Ok.

Cherish me like I'm precious and temporary. Like, I could be destroyed if handled with nothing less than the utmost care. And at the same time, I want to be *seen* as dope, intelligent, sensual, carefree. I want to be **wanted**. I want to be **necessary**. I never was before. And now, it appears, **I am**.

Right next to me, the one I've waited for. Someone I didn't seek out or lose bits of myself to appease. He's right here next to me within the short reach of my fingers. The pad of my index grazes his hip. He doesn't move. It's like he's used to me reaching out in the early moments of dawn, reassuring myself that he's right there. Within reach. For me. For us. I was so tired of depending on my daughter to be my safe place. My sanctuary. My laughter and daylight in the darkest of nights. She was always enough to bring about smiles and provide warmth through the thousand watts of her smile or the complete and utter perfection of her hugs. My child, my heartbeat, my dream come true. She was always enough. But it wasn't her job to complete my happiness, it was mine. I couldn't keep putting the responsibility of a joy investment on her. I love her, and she loves me. But I needed to find love within myself.

That was the hard part. Telling myself, I was good enough. Pretty enough. Tall enough. Thick enough. Yes, <u>thick enough.</u> It tends to be important whether we want it to be or not. But, to bring about the love I am required to feel about myself, I absolutely had to find some things to be vain about.

So, let me *choose* my hips and my ass.

I've never had an issue with the kinks in my hair or my brown skin. Cute is what I'm called, but it was never enough to jumpstart my self-romance. Self-romances went beyond caring about everything external, which should have been easy, easy peasy. It wasn't. I had to learn that my character was never an issue. It was never *truly* me. It was the cliche. When I was discarded and told, "It's not you; it's me." I should've believed it. I might have been being thrown a line at the time, but it carried weight.

It was accurate. **I am great!** I deserved more than fickle contemplations of what a relationship should have been. I was worthy of more than lies, cheating, and total disregard of my feelings. My feelings were valid. **Valid as fuck!** And once I realized that and took a deep look at myself, the person <u>I am</u> and not what people want me to be, I found that I am everything!

I AM EVERYTHING!

And realizing this shifted my world view, making me want what I deserved instead of settling for what was handed to me. I think the change allowed me to see what was real instead of what I once saw through those dirty rose-colored glasses. The prior view was shitty. I don't know why I even wore them. I HATE roses! I digress.

I'm lying here, in this bed, with this man, the man who loves me with everything he has. The things he lacks, he strives to get. He finally shifts into the gentle pressure of my touch and turns to his side, eyes still closed. He takes my hand from his hip and places it to his lips, pressing a kiss. He places my hand on his chest and draws lazy circles on the back of it. I sigh. Two words escape his lips into the air that I know, with certainty, will be done each and every rotation of the sun "Good Morning. "

And it is, finally.

B. Wet Dreams

wet dream
/ˈˌwet ˈdrēm/

noun

1: an erotic dream culminating in orgasm and in the male accompanied by ejaculation of semen
2: an exceedingly pleasurable or exciting experience, situation, or fantasy

June 18

If I cannot be with you
Or
Get to you
I will use the absence to
Dream of you
The space that lies between us
Leaves my love unaffected
I crave you
Not for the things you do
But
The things beneath my skin
My pulse
Controlled by you
Remotely
The battery of your voice
The synergy of your words
Affect me
Almost as much as
Kisses on skin
The way you sink your
Fingers in
Wetness
I say your name
I ache for your kiss
My tongue dancing with yours
My tongue between your lips
Below your hips
Your rise
My favorite mouthpiece
It's absolute
I need you
The desire I have
Jumpstarts each
Nerve ending
Making each movement
A signete of your name
June 18

SENRYU

I

I dream in crimson
Emerging from love's caress
Turning smiles to moans

II

Your target my throat
Consuming a feast of butter
Nothing is sweeter

III

Hands around my waist
your body fills mine with strength
I can't let you go

TANKA

I want to surround
My lips about the layered
Manor of your well
Swallowing the waters of
Your want. Fill my appetite.

My Fantasy

      let me
I'm feeling you.
How many times must I express?
Infinite numbers?
Damn, can't you see?
"I'm feenin'"
What part don't you understand?
      let me
      let me lay you down
      let me *love* you
      let me taste you
      let me
      turn you *IN*.
            Don't wanna turn you *OUT*
            I want this shit for keeps
      let me
      let me extend one leg
      top to bottom
      be a magician
      switchin' tricks
      acrobatics and shit
            party in my lap!
      spin around
      dance around
      do circles
      all in it
If I get one more
Singular moment
Of your affection,
I would make it last
An eternity.
      swallow the shit
      hmmmm
      let me

C. Nightmare on Elm St.

night·mare on elm street
/ˈnītˌmer 'än,ôn 'elm 'strēt/

And now I lay me down to sleep,
 I pray the Lord, my soul, to keep.
And if I die before I wake,
 I pray the Lord, my soul, to take.

"Sticks and stones may break my bones,
but nothing will ever kill me. Well, let's
see now. First, they tried burning me.
Then they tried burying me. But this…
this is my favorite. They even tried Holy
water! But I just keep on tickin'…
because they promised me that.
  - *Freddy Kruger*
  Freddy's Dead: The Final Nightmare 1991

"Why are you screaming when
I haven't even cut you yet?"
  - *Freddy Krueger*
  A Nightmare On Elmstreet. 2010

Acknowledgement of Misery

I see darkness that
Won't transpose to light.
My heart,
Restless.

What more can a prisoner
Of my own knowledge,
A self chained slave,
Hope for?

My once open door,
An exit closed hard.
My smile replaced
By anguished sounds.

My joy,
Once long-lasting,
Quickly dissipated by your
Lack of understanding.

Reflecting on
Moments,
Thieved glances,
And wishes.

The reciprocation
Bartered by penny thrown,
With eyes closed
Into a fountain.

Hoping for things
That cannot
Be obtained.
Fools' Gold.

Biding my time for the
Confusing truth to be
Revealed between us three.
You, me, and uncertainty.

Truth must take
The bolder role.
It won't.
Time has alluded us.
My mind allows the threat
Of the unknown and the
Danger of pre-conceived thoughts
To make me it's home.

For too long,
Gloom corrupted
My sing-laugh-smile.
I'm changed irrefutably.

Who knew
Someone's passing
Could derail
My entire train of thought.

Departing and taking with you
Unanswered questions.
Selfishly denying me
Promised closure.

Body left cold and silent
Taking what I wanted
For myself
And locking it in a box

Buried 6 feet.
Leaving me alone
In the knowledge
Of my misery.

Missing You

It's not the same
  when you're not here

The sadness comes
  when you're away

The sun is dim
  when you're not here

Not brightly lit
  when you're away

My hearts not whole
  when you're not here

It stays broken
  when you're away

I want you back
  when you're not here

It hurts me deep
  when you're away

Masters-Son

As I greet you with open arms
You bear me no smile
You look my way
My heart folds, fades away
I speak to you; you don't speak back
You show your love to others
Leaving me to hang my head
And feel nothing but grief
I can't touch nor reach you

You act as though I am not there
You turn away from the sight of me
And kill my soul
I didn't mean what I might have done
To cause this distance between us
If I could have your presence
If I could only have you back
My heart would be lifted
And I would have eternal joy

I'm sorry

Rav'n

that smile
voice of an angel
held within
not yet bold
enough to share
only a child
innocent
laughter as a
bell chime passed
through distant winds

i wonder
what could have been
it's over
you're gone now
an emptiness fills
the bed where
you lay
i place my hand
where i felt
your essence
we were shareholders
in life
i feeding you
you feeling me
me feeling filled
by you
my glow is gone
as you are

Silence

Lives are empty spaces
With nowhere to go
Transparent slaves to sorrow
Inside
Our hearts are breaking
But still
Our lives carry on
With silence distilling
The lonely heart
Which feeds upon itself
Hopeless

SENRYU

I

Take away this pain
Holding my head for hours
Closing my eyes now

II

I hide how I feel
To protect those around me
My thoughts are not kind

III

I am tired of
Speaking and not being heard
Please listen to me

IV

Death is my best friend
Not my own but your demise
Keeps my soul at peace

V

I protected you
For you to hurt and betray
You didn't love me

VI

The sight of your blood
Draining from wounds, they can't stop
Makes me smile. Giggle

Take it Back!

Take it back!
Tell me it's not true
Tell me I'm still with you
Wrap your arms around me
Say I love you

Take it back!
Tell me I'm still yours
Tell me I'm what your heart beats for
Wrap your arms around
Say I need you

Take it back!
Kiss these tears away
Make love night and day
Wrap your arms around me
Say I want you

Take it back!
Wake me from this hell
Make the end a fairy tale
Wrap your arms around me
Say I take you back
8.22.01

9-29-01

You lied to me.

Dear,

    Why do I insist on believing? Why can't I follow what my head is telling me? Is it that I'm a fool in love? Or That I can't get enough of you? Should I really try and stick to everything I feel? Does that mean I will still be hurting? Will I be lonely, still?

    What makes me think I can trust you? (*Other than the fact that I love you and you say you love me too.*) I believe if you needed me like you want me to believe, you wouldn't hurt me like you do.

    I go around covering my eyes to everything you say and do. So desperate when it comes to attention from you.

I sit and wait up in my bed for you. I cry at night from the absence of you. I want so much for you to want me too. I don't' ask questions for the answers I want from you. Cause I'm scared of losing you.

I love you. What should I do?

Signed

Losing faith in you

Shook

I stood in this busy space. Spicy aromas, background noises, people seated in meetings, eating their dinners, free and at peace filled the air.

I, oblivious to everything but the smell of freshly baked bread, waited for my turn. A red light and vibration on a disk captured my attention. I put it in the basket, trading it for a bag of happy; turn on heel and head to exit.

A hand grabs my arm; I excuse myself thinking I've traveled too fast, not paying attention, and maybe got in the way. Or maybe I left something, dropped something. But I hadn't.

Purse on shoulder, bag in hand, I looked up and lost my footing. My stomach instantly unsettled.

Shook

My favorite place now a new hazard no longer safe.

> *Too close to home.*
> *You are too close to me.*
> *You shouldn't be here.*
> *You shouldn't see me.*
> *Your eyes shouldn't wander.*
> *They shouldn't have lit up!*
> *They are dirty.*
> *They fester.*
> *You still have my arm.*

Shook

I shook you off, scene or no scene, scream or no scream.

> *You can't be here!*
> *You can't touch me!*
> *Not again!*
> *NEVER again!*

The tomb in your face opens to spill whatever death resides
on that tongue. I swat at the air with my left hand, trying to deflect
whatever rotting entity spews in my ears' direction
I clutch my bag in my right hand, forcing my feet not to run.
I make haste wishing that left arm stayed with you instead of still attached, burning from another touch you had no permission to give.

Shook

You say my name; it bounces against the closing of doors. You say my name; it falls apart like air aged bread, poorly concocted lies, and honeymooned thighs. You say my name, and it propelled me to exit.

I'm now The Flash. I am now competing with the speed of light from counter to closed doors.

I run to my car.
I lock my doors.
I start my engine.
I back out.
I barely miss a car
I barely miss the ice
I barely miss a collision
I drive.
I can't breathe.

I still have a fire on my left arm. My eyes fill up with anger, fear, helplessness.

The empty promises of what would be said and what I would do are in complete opposition of reality.

I cry.
I keep crying.

Shook

This Ain't Oz

Keep fuckin with me; I'll get you my pretty and your little bitch too!

I have purposely stayed distant, clamped my arms to my sides, nails dug into palms to suppress the shaking that starts from the tips of my fingers, cutting the inside flesh. I need to see your blood hot, pulsating as it rushes from the 3 or 4 wounds that gape seeping air and steam as your life escapes.

I want it. Hot. At my feet. On my shoes. On my hands as they arrive to question me. Eyes wide, jaws dropped, they feel queasy. Notepads open but pens still unsure of where to start.

I have pictured it a few ways. Never a gun, bludgeoned. It's a fav word; it's such a fun word. I love how you have to use every bit of your mouth to say it. Lips pressed. Tip of tongue touches roof of mouth right at teeth then falls back down to the bottom row. So, the d sound can connect with a tap. The action is way more than a tap.

> *Beating with a blunt,*
> *heavy object rendering*
> *unconscious until dead.*

Forensics would have a field day with the splatter patterns, a museum of Rorschach. What will you see? A butterfly? Summer sky? Fall leaves, presumably oak? That's the shape most often identified. Will that be the final image that will seal my fate from bashing your face?

> *Bones crush,*
> *skin caves, bends.*
> *Pulp.*

The cliché bloody pulp. Bloody, it's how I see you. Not with my hands. They don't have the wingspan needed to stop your breathing successfully, but, it's more intimate that way. It's sexy, gripping a throat, but it's not as effective when the result needs death. You have to use the crook of your arm and lean back, allowing their weight to steady yours, leaving the placement of their airflow empty. Joints are potent tools. Remember what a knee can do to take a breath away? A well-placed arm can do the same. But it's not as artistic as the plastic bag combo.

Tied tight, pulled.
Eyes bug.
Feet kick.
Face becomes
a kaleidoscope of colors.

Eyes erupt in vessels never seen before. The proper word for it is beautiful. Strangle is as ugly as it sounds, but asphyxiation, say it again, asphyxiation. The five syllables of that beautiful word take longer than knife wounds, but less messy.

Pause.

You do realize this whole journey through thought was brought about by you? It was generated from conversations about you and things I'm not allowed to do. Of course, these things aren't beyond my means. However, they would hurt, within a matter of seconds, the hearts attached to people who love me. They don't like me like this.

Un-pause.
The knife wounds
are just as messy
as the prior topic
of your beating.

Maybe, even more, depending on the blade stopping you mid-stride, spearpoint. I need to make an example of you. To do this, I'd need a Gut hook. Skinning you requires a trailing point. But, I don't need anything special to put you down and destroy every bit of what holds you together, rip you apart. You aren't worth the time it takes.

The repeated thrusts into your flesh will make me have to do more … work. I don't want to have to wash my hands, ruin my clothes. At the same time, I would JUST TO SHUT YOUR MOUTH! I need silence from the shit you do and say, the way you treat people, the life you live. Your life burdens me. I see you dead, but not instantly. The screams, the struggle, I close my eyes and see it clearly. When I open them up, it's back to reality. You are still here, and I remember me and what brought me here. But…

Keep fuckin with me;
I'll get you my pretty
and your little bitch too!

D. Ror·schach test

Ror·schach
/ˈrôrˌSHäk ˌtest/

noun

a type of projective test used in psychoanalysis, in which a standard set of symmetrical inkblots of different shapes and colors is presented one by one to the subject, who is asked to describe what they suggest or resemble; analyzed as an indication of personality traits, preoccupations and conflicts.

Lend A Hand

I wish I could fill your shoes man
Take away all your blues man
The truth is I can't
I hate what all this is doing to you
Seems like no one gets
What you're going through
But between me and you
If no one else understands
Please know
I do
If the life tree could
Use a branch or two and
Turn it into a switch
Like the grandmothers do
I'm sure they could
Forcibly move generations
Have them waking in line
Into a prelude of lifetimes
We could reverse
The transitional flow
Make it how shit's
Really supposed to go
Take all hardships and
Make every struggle better
Start things over
New
If I had any power
I would do that for you
I'd do all I can
Just to lend a hand

Ok Then

So,
call it special circumstances
that I agreed to write.
Such requests many times before
by others have been ignored.
So,
if and when you choose
to respond, take note:
I need no reminder of the ties
that already bind
when my muse whispers to me.

SENRYU

I

I love Soul Sessions
Simmy Is an awesome host
I thank God for Mark

II

Reincarnation
Someone tell me this is real
Need another chance

III

Jill Scott and Bilal
I wore a sexy blue dress
He wasn't worth it

TANKA

I sing from my heart
melodies mean so much more
creates space to heal
keys drums bass filling my soul
I lean in and bless the mic

The Question

I try to live
live my life
the way I should

seems like all i do
does not do
anyone no good

cause what happens is
9x's out of 10
it goes unknown

but still I "be"
the best at me
don't care if public's shown

with you it seems
it seems as though
my *all* is in vain

I know you want
the best of me
and yet you still refrain

I try so hard
so hard to please
please each elements' forte

but now I see
I must please me
from me I cannot stray

So,
if i was to try
to try and
give my all

would I be here
be waiting here
unmoved for every call

Baby Tate

It's hard to believe I'm in the same world I was in just a few moons ago. What I conceive as a notion of peace has grown beyond thoughts of creativity. My world has grown into an Ephesus of tranquility pulsating with hope.

At last, I see your smile. Finally, I feel equality within the measures of my heart. I love being around you even more so now.

You have recovered a piece of my soul.

I thank you for that.

Difficult

Some people try to understand
The confusing things I do
I hardly try to set them straight
I couldn't if I tried to

A Missing Angel

I can see you
Can you see me?
I see me.
I see me no you.
Look
I's not me
It's not me, not me
Me not me.
You not you.
You & Me?
Me not with you.
No you with me.
Just you.
Me with me.
Just me.
You with you, not with me.
I'm not me without you.
Without you, there's no me

8.24.01

It's a good feeling to sit
Amid a plethora of
Women
Colors | Shapes | Sizes
Skin
Red Mahogany | Autumn Leaf Yellow
Hair
Flips | Bobs | Shags | Hair Weave | Micros | Parts | Afros | Twists
The sashay in the platformed switch
The white-painted toenail
The gossips itch
A circle of new friends
I sit between the beauty of
Sisterhood and laughter,
Intermingled with pink and green.
Filled with wonderment,
The light of smiles welcomes.
If I could just be a part,
This feeling I have will forever
Lay within my heart.
The vibe is strong in here *for real*.
The music of voices fills my ear.
I'm diggin' this!
It's not too often I get a chance
To be among sistas
For more than circumstance

Hopefully,
I will get to *know*.
Make new friends.
Let kinships grow.

ESPN Balla-Wanna-Be

look at y'all
getting' all sweaty
runnin' back and forth
like y'all can ball
it's no wonder
ain't nare one of y'all
shootin' 3's
too busy shootin' off
at the mouth
to fulfill any real
hoop dreams
always talkin' 'bout
  "Watch me break some ankles."
nigga please!
with lay-ups like these
ya be doin' well
to scrape a knee
watchin' old-timers
make y'all eat dirt
while ya usin' excuses
  "My leg, my back, my wrist hurt!"
cussin' at real ball playa's
  "I got fouled!"
need to pay attention
to ya sorry ass game
cause ya know ya wild'n out
same old brotha runnin' round
tryna to do his thing
need to take his
sad ass home
and keep them
hoop dreams
in the screen

Here

Under a navy velvet sky
I sit,
Just me
Among ten thousand oak
Or was it sarsaparilla?
I find comfort within
September breeze
And too many lights
Among grass
To catch a glimpse of
More than three stars
Too many cars on the street
To hear grasshoppers, June bugs or
Any other creature
Nature's replacement
Concrete walls of fancy
A park
Not woods
Still
I find comfort
Here

Dragonfly

I long for dragonflies while locked away in these stone gray walls. I sit in hushed thought, void lighted prisms, and distorted hues. How ordinary it must be to live a butterfly's life. Their simple beauty, always seen. Colors pleasant, constant. *Always, always, always.*

    Who pays attention to the magnificence of a Dragonfly?

Wings transparent
Rainbows of metallic wonder
Black body arrow straight
Wishing for rain
Wanting for waters
Afton | Shenandoah | The Nile
Bodies to create a home
Blue-green | Muddy brown | Crystal clear

I'd circle the bayou,
Mingle with the gator,
Hide among the willow,
Zim, Zim.
Ah to fly!
No one as beautiful as I.
Me, greater than the
Lowly butterfly.
Distinct in feature.
Mystic in nature.

I open my eyes while relishing the thought. Return to these four walls to sit in my blue chair, longing for dragonflies.

Women

Silly women
Cryin women
Always lyin' women
Scandalous women
Always trippin' women
I'm not trying' to step to your man women
I'm not buyin' but I'm sellin' women
Lifes a job women
In my face women
Want what I got but ain't got what it takes women
Needy women
Independent women
Can't stand what you about women
Face scarred women
Dance on bars women
Perm or weave women
Platinum dye women
HIV survived women
Booty shorts women
Breast hang all out women
Prude and one-man women
Everybody's man and dick suckin' women
Can't be or live without a man women
Can't keep friends with any other women, women
Don't like men women
Don't fuck men women
Women who love women
Gold digging women
Sugar baby women
Dominatrix women
Submissive women
Spend paychecks on nice fits women but
Ain't fed them kids women
Too young to be on welfare women
Too old to be working women
Rainbow mothering women
Barren Women
I don't even want children women
Smile in my face talk behind my back women

Always wanting a 2nd, 3rd, and 4th chance women
Never apologetic women
I said what I said women
Transwomen women
Domestic violence women
Sexual assaulted women
Conceal and Carry women
Little ponytail you know they can fight women
Cancer Survivor women
Amputee women
In the military or veteran women
Entrepreneur women
Singing women
Writing women
Preaching women
Praying Women
Pagan casting spells women
Wear my zodiac sign around my neck women
Juggling streams of income women
Educated on stocks and bonds women
Getting that degree women
PWI or HBCU women
Homeless women
Jet setting women
Advocating women
Silent and to yourself women
So many more women
A multitude of hued women
There is nothing that exists
Or can be of any quality without
Women

Leaving Home

This bus is moving

Moving to a place where
I might learn something
Heading to a place where
My heart might mend
Heading to peace of mind
Moving
I look to my left at the traffic
Watching the trees move fast as light
I close my eyes
Concentrate on my body
Moving
Beat and rhythm of wheels
Engine rumbling my ear

This bus is moving

Moving to a place where a woman
No longer fears love's brutality
Moving to a place where a woman
No longer fears her husband's hits
Moving to a place where someone is
Anxious for a winter's summer
Palm trees and ocean waters
Miami
Heading towards a sick mother or father
I look to my right
A tall black man with skin like night
Rests his head and closes his eyes
All in the groove of the bus' move

This bus is moving

Discovery

I dream discovery.

Realizing
there is
something
new
not seen
heard
spoken
A new day

I want to
know
learn
speak
share
the unseen
the unknown
I miss sharing

What I've had, I've held close.
Alone.

Not Quite a Bucket List

I love being barefoot
Toes grabbing rug
Pushing tile
Moving grass
I'll pick up a penny
Pull back a blanket

I love eating candy
Caramel, chewy, fruity,
Nutty, chocolate goodness
Never minding that extra pound
For the exchange of a chew
Or two

I savor a good book
Create my mood,
Ignite the flare of
Imagination that
Sweeps me to a distant land
Time or idea

I long to Dance
Enjoy the attention
Can stop an entire crowd
With one hip slip
Feeling the beat
Beneath these feet

I long to kiss
Slow long and soft
Tender wetness
Drum beat to my heart
Taste my mind's imagined love
The intimacy of lip to lip

I want to run
Crazy rush
Feel strong again
Passing the limits of
A sidewalk and street

To infinity

I dream of swimming
Imagining backstroke skills
Doggy paddles
And diving
Envisioning green algae
And sea mammoth

I envision all these things

I love
I savor
I long
I want
I dream
I do
I am
I try
        I will

My Origin Story

I started off as sound
A series of notes
A chord
Like in that
Hallelujah song
With the major 5th?
I apparently please the Lord

And it makes sense
I'm made of music
It flows from me
There is no way
I could be
Anything but
Melody

It's just a matter
Of pinpointing
Whether I traveled
Through the
Metals of windchimes
Or the tinkering
Of an old piano

My sound has no sight
I could have
Seeped from
Water filled
Wine glasses,
Hit with the silver
Of teaspoons…

Or the voices of
Little white boys who
Are required to eliminate
Vibrato and sing
Wholly straight notes

On stage at
Carnegie Hall

I just know I was sound

I fell like rain upon
The faces of children
That know heirs
Hair can't get wet
And get
Beat like drums
In a faraway land

Tribes use me
Need me
I am communication
I am celebration
Before I was born
I was the muse of many
And the desire of one

I started off as sound
A great sound
I just don't know how
I was formed
But how ever it came
I still managed
To be heard

Tigerlilystar is an emerging writer most recently featured in "Black Imagination." Curated by Natasha Marin. Hailing from Kansas City, she is a multidisciplinary creative performing artist that also dances and sings. Best described as a woman's woman, Tigerlilystar uses her pen to articulate the depth and struggle of womanhood while having the courage and honesty to admit wanting love and going after it. Brave enough to walk her own path, she is an eclectic pool of originality and fantasy that allows readers to search the nice and not so nice parts of the human psyche.

@tigerlilystar

www.ingramcontent.com/pod-product-compliance
Lightning Source LLC
Chambersburg PA
CBHW030347100526
44592CB00010B/866